SUMMARY OF SECRETS TO STEWARDING GOD'S VOICE IN A NEW ERA

The Power and Price of Influence

JEREMIAH JOHNSON

DESTINY IMAGE

All emphasis within Scripture quotations is the author's own. Please note that Destiny Image's publishing style capitalizes certain pronouns in Scripture that refer to the Father, Son, and Holy Spirit, and may differ from some publishers' styles. Take note that the name satan and related names are not capitalized. We choose not to acknowledge him, even to the point of violating grammatical rules.

Destiny Image P.O. Box 310, Shippensburg, PA 17257-0310

This book and all other Destiny Image's books are available at Christian bookstores and distributors worldwide.

For Worldwide Distribution.

Reach us on the Internet: www.destinyimage.com.

ISBN 13 TP: 9798881500757

ISBN 13 eBook: 9798881500764

CONTENTS

INTRODUCTION

INTRODUCTION: SUMMARY OF SECRETS TO STEWARDING GOD'S VOICE IN A NEW ERA

In an age marked by rapid technological advancements and profound cultural shifts, the necessity for believers to discern and steward the voice of God remains more crucial than ever. "Secrets to Stewarding God's Voice in a New Era" offers an essential guide for navigating this dynamic landscape, ensuring that Christians not only hear but also effectively respond to God's directives amidst the noise of the modern world.

This summary distills the core insights from the original book, providing readers with a concise yet comprehensive overview of the principles and practices vital for maintaining a clear channel to divine guidance. It is designed as a practical toolkit that bridges timeless biblical wisdom with contemporary challenges, enabling believers to apply God's wisdom practically in their daily lives.

As we delve into the summary, you will be introduced to strategies that enhance spiritual perception, including fostering a life of prayer and meditation, understanding the role of the Holy Spirit in divine communication, and cultivating a heart posture that aligns with God's purposes. The summary emphasizes the transformative power of aligning one's life with God's word and the peace that comes from assured divine guidance.

Moreover, this summary highlights the importance of community and accountability in the process of discerning God's voice. It explores how relationships within the Body of Christ can support personal growth and ensure that one's interpretation of divine messages remains on solid theological ground.

Through this exploration, "Secrets to Stewarding God's Voice in a New Era" equips you to step confidently into your calling with the assurance that God's voice leads your decisions and actions. Whether you are a seasoned believer or new to your faith journey, this summary aims to invigorate your spiritual practices and enhance your responsiveness to the divine voice that speaks into the complexities of life today.

Prepare to deepen your understanding and expand your ability to operate in the realm of spiritual discernment as we navigate the insights of "Secrets to Stewarding God's Voice in a New Era." This summary promises to be both enlightening and empowering, offering you the keys to effectively communicate with God in a world that is constantly changing.

CHAPTER 1

THE SECRET TO INFLUENCE AND LEGACY

Bible Verse

"John answered and said, 'A man can receive nothing unless it has been given to him from heaven.'" - John 3:27 (NKJV)

Introduction

This chapter delves into the profound realization that influence carries not only great responsibility but also significant personal costs. It explores the spiritual and personal challenges that come with public prominence, drawing from both biblical examples and the author's experiences.

Word of Wisdom

"The truth is that if we do not crucify our flesh privately, our flesh will crucify us publicly!" Jeremiah Johnson

. . .

Main Theme

The main theme of this chapter focuses on understanding and managing the power and price of influence in a spiritual and ethical manner, with an emphasis on integrity, humility, and the constant need for divine guidance.

Key Points

- Influence is both a privilege and a burden, requiring careful stewardship and personal sacrifice.
- Biblical figures like King Uzziah and Saul illustrate how public influence can lead to personal downfall if not managed with humility.
- Influence should be seen as a tool given by God for specific Kingdom purposes, as shown in the lives of Esther and Samuel.
- John the Baptist exemplifies the ideal balance of influence, combining clarity of message with personal humility.
- Maintaining a simple lifestyle and a focus on servanthood helps protect against the corruption that influence can bring.
- The greatest influence is achieved by those who seek not their own fame, but the glory of Jesus Christ.

Key Themes

- **Responsibility and Testing:** Influence comes with intense scrutiny and spiritual testing, where one's character and faith are continually challenged. Leaders must discern between tests from God meant to refine them and attacks from adversaries meant to derail them.

- **The Dual Edge of Influence:** As influence grows, so does the likelihood of facing both internal and external challenges, including jealousy, slander, and the temptation to abuse power. Leaders must manage these pressures while maintaining their spiritual and moral integrity.
- **Spiritual Stewardship:** True influence requires recognizing it as a gift from God meant for specific purposes. This perspective encourages a focus on divine rather than personal agendas, as demonstrated by figures like Esther and Samuel who used their positions to fulfill God's plans.
- **The Model of John the Baptist:** John's life highlights the ideal use of influence—strong in conviction, unwavering in the face of opposition, and humble in spirit, always pointing others to Christ rather than seeking personal gain.
- **The Legacy of Humility and Service:** The enduring influence is not marked by numbers or fame, but by the depth of commitment to serving God and others. This is seen in the impactful, albeit humble, ministries of historical figures like John Wesley and George Whitefield who prioritized Christ over personal recognition.

Conclusion

Influence is a powerful but dangerous tool that, when harnessed with godly wisdom and humility, can lead to significant spiritual impact. However, it demands a high moral and spiritual discipline to prevent the personal pitfalls that have ensnared many. Leaders are called to steward their influence carefully, ensuring their legacy aligns with God's purposes, fostering a deep, lasting impact that glorifies God above all.

CHAPTER 2

DON'T DESPISE YOUR YOUTH

Bible Verse

"Let no one despise your youth, but be an example to the believers in word, in conduct, in love, in spirit, in faith, in purity." - 1 Timothy 4:12 (NKJV)

Introduction

This chapter reflects on the early years of the author's ministry, starting from the age of 12, through the trials and humble beginnings of serving in overlooked places, to achieving widespread influence. It emphasizes the importance of faithfulness and humility in ministry.

Word of Wisdom

"The truth is that many of us have to serve a Saul to get the Saul out of us!" Jeremiah Johnson

. . .

Main Theme

The primary theme is the cultivation of genuine influence through humble service and steadfast faithfulness, starting from a young age and in challenging environments.

Key Points

- The author began ministering to the needy at a young age, setting a foundation for future opportunities.
- Early ministry involved preaching in less glamorous settings like prisons and retirement parks, emphasizing service over recognition.
- Encounters with God during periods of intense service shaped the author's future and expanded his influence.
- Ministry success is attributed to divine appointments and faithful stewardship rather than personal ambition.
- The author warns of the dangers of entitlement and pride that often accompany growing influence.
- True influence requires a foundation of character, tested through service and humility.

Key Themes

- **Foundational Experiences in Ministry:** Early experiences of ministering in challenging environments are crucial for spiritual growth. These humble beginnings keep one grounded and prepare one for greater responsibilities.
- **The Danger of Entitlement in Ministry:** As influence grows, so does the temptation to feel entitled. The author emphasizes that genuine ministry should focus on service rather than personal gain, warning against the seductions of fame and recognition.
- **Divine Encounters as Turning Points:** Key moments of divine intervention are highlighted as turning points in the author's ministry. These encounters directed his path and expanded his influence beyond his initial expectations.
- **Stewardship of Influence:** Influence is portrayed as a gift from God that must be carefully managed. The author stresses that influence should be used to glorify God and serve others, not to boost one's ego.
- **Pitfalls of Public Ministry:** Public ministry comes with its trials, including criticism, misunderstanding, and spiritual warfare. The author shares personal stories of navigating these challenges, underscoring the need for continuous humility and reliance on God.

Conclusion

The journey to meaningful influence in ministry is fraught with challenges that test one's character and commitment to God's purpose. By embracing humility, enduring trials, and focusing on serving others, one can truly make a lasting impact that honors God. The author's life serves as a testament to the power of starting small, remaining faithful, and allowing God to lead the way in ministry.

CHAPTER 3

THE DANGERS OF CELEBRITY CHRISTIANITY

Bible Verse

"Blessed are the poor in spirit, for theirs is the kingdom of heaven." – Matthew 5:3 (NIV)

Introduction

In a time where influence and celebrity culture are infiltrating the Church, the chapter "The Dangers of Celebrity Christianity" highlights the pressing need for believers to return to humility, spiritual integrity, and devotion to God. The chapter discusses the temptations that come with platform and fame, the essential distinction between true leadership and superficial popularity, and the urgency of preserving the purity of the gospel in a culture obsessed with image and success.

Word of Wisdom

"Never allow the size of your platform to change your message! You must refuse to be bought!" Jeremiah Johnson

Main Theme

This chapter challenges the growing trend of celebrity culture within the Church, calling for leaders and believers to focus on spiritual integrity, humility, and obedience to God rather than seeking fame, influence, or public approval.

Key Points

- The global Church is undergoing a period of exposure, shaking, and necessary division to separate those who truly stand for biblical truth from those who compromise for popularity.
- Celebrity Christianity has become a form of idol worship, with many church leaders tempted by fame, money, and influence at the expense of the gospel.
- Some influential Christian leaders encourage compromising messages, especially on controversial issues such as abortion, sexual immorality, and holiness.
- True leaders must resist the temptation to water down the gospel for greater influence and instead embrace repentance, holiness, and integrity.

- Celebrity Christianity is dangerous as it places more importance on platform and public approval than intimacy with God.
- Humility, exemplified by being "poor in spirit," is key to avoiding the pitfalls of celebrity culture in the Church.

Key Themes

- **Spiritual Division for Unity**: The author explains that God is allowing division within the Church to expose hidden sins and to bring true unity based on adherence to biblical truth. This division will separate those who seek truth from those who prioritize worldly approval.
- **The Dangers of Celebrity Christianity**: The chapter addresses the rise of celebrity culture among Christian leaders, where fame, influence, and platforms become idols. This shift prioritizes appearance over substance, leading to compromised messages.
- **Refusing to Compromise the Gospel**: Leaders face pressure to soften their messages to appeal to larger audiences, especially regarding difficult topics like repentance and sexual immorality. However, the author emphasizes the importance of remaining true to the gospel, no matter the cost.
- **Addiction to Ministry**: Pursuing ministry platforms for personal gain, rather than for serving God, has become a hidden addiction in the Church. Leaders can get

caught up in networking, popularity, and open doors, using ministry as a cover for personal dysfunction.

- **Humility and Character**: The chapter stresses that God is more interested in a leader's character and humility than in their influence. True spiritual leaders are called to serve and walk in humility, prioritizing prayer, devotion, and godly character over celebrity.

Conclusion

In a culture where fame and influence are often pursued, the Church must remain vigilant against the dangers of celebrity Christianity. True leaders in the Kingdom of God will resist the temptation to compromise for the sake of popularity, instead choosing humility, integrity, and intimacy with God. The ultimate calling is to serve Christ and His people, not to seek personal glory or recognition. Through humility and faithfulness, the Church can stand firm in its witness to the world.

CHAPTER 4

HEALTHY COMMUNITY AND ACCOUNTABILITY

Bible Verse

"Let us consider how we may spur one another on toward love and good deeds, not giving up meeting together, as some are in the habit of doing, but encouraging one another—and all the more as you see the Day approaching." - Hebrews 10:24-25 (NIV)

Introduction

This chapter discusses the critical role of a supportive, truthful community and accountability in sustaining long-term success and integrity for individuals with significant influence. It warns against the isolation that often accompanies rising fame and influence.

Word of Wisdom

"Making money and becoming famous

is not the goal of following Jesus." Jeremiah Johnson

Main Theme

The main theme centers on the importance of surrounding oneself with a community that offers genuine support and accountability, which safeguards against moral and spiritual failures.

Key Points

- Influence can lead to both positive impacts and significant failures depending on one's support system.
- The local church plays a crucial role in providing community and accountability.
- True accountability involves people who know the real you, not just the public persona.
- It's vital to differentiate between temporary impact and lasting spiritual fruit in one's ministry.
- Having people who can vouch for one's character is essential for genuine leadership.

Key Themes

- **The Role of the Local Church:** The local church is not just a place of worship but a community that provides essential grounding and accountability for its members, especially those in leadership. This support is vital for maintaining integrity and humility, as it provides leaders with a platform to be themselves and receive honest feedback and guidance.

- **Distinguishing Impact from Fruit:** It's important to recognize the difference between short-term impact and long-term spiritual fruit. While traveling ministries can influence many temporarily, the consistent, day-to-day involvement in a local community reveals true spiritual growth and character.
- **Challenges of Online and Traveling Ministries:** Ministers who are constantly traveling or who are heavily involved in online ministries may lack genuine, deep connections with a home community, which can lead to a lack of accountability and a skewed perception of one's own character and effectiveness.
- **The Necessity of Discernment and Accountability:** Effective accountability requires discernment—recognizing who genuinely supports you versus who may be seeking their own benefit. This discernment is crucial in forming a circle of trust that contributes positively to one's spiritual and personal development.
- **Consequences of Isolation in Leadership:** Leaders who isolate themselves from a community or resist accountability often face moral and spiritual declines. This isolation can result

from the deceitful allure of independence
that fame and influence bring.

Conclusion

The pathway to sustaining influence and success in any field, especially ministry, is deeply rooted in the community and accountability. Leaders must actively seek and maintain connections with those who will provide honest feedback, share in their spiritual journey, and keep them grounded in their faith and personal life. This chapter serves as a reminder of the dangers of navigating influence without a strong, supportive community and the blessings of remaining connected and accountable.

CHAPTER 5

OVERCOMING JEALOUSY

Bible Verse

"For where you have envy and selfish ambition, there you find disorder and every evil practice." - James 3:16 (NIV)

Introduction

This chapter explores the pervasive issue of jealousy, particularly how it affects those with influence. It highlights the destructiveness of jealousy and provides strategies for navigating and overcoming this challenge.

Word of Wisdom

"Remember, satan uses people to attack, criticize, and question pioneers so that those who are getting set free, refreshed, and empowered by their life and ministry will become confused, disoriented,

and altogether stop listening to the emerging pioneers." Jeremiah Johnson

Main Theme

The main theme delves into the dangers of jealousy in leadership and influence, emphasizing the importance of maintaining humility and integrity in the face of envy from others.

Key Points

- Jealousy is a serious sin that leads to destructive behaviors.
- Historical biblical figures and Jesus himself faced jealousy despite their humility.
- Jealousy can come from both close acquaintances and strangers.
- Overcoming jealousy requires acceptance that it cannot be completely avoided.
- Criticisms from others often stem from their own jealousy.
- Navigating jealousy is essential for fulfilling one's destiny without being undermined.

Key Themes

- **Inevitability and Impact of Jealousy:** Regardless of one's demeanor or humility, jealousy is an inevitable part of having influence. It can manifest in harmful ways, including personal attacks and attempts to undermine one's character and achievements.

- **Misunderstanding Due to Jealousy:** Many misunderstandings and conflicts are rooted in jealousy, with detractors often misinterpreting the actions and words of those they envy. Recognizing this can help leaders avoid unnecessary conflicts and focus on their mission.
- **Strategies to Handle Jealousy:** Leaders need to develop strategies to handle jealousy, including fostering a culture of celebration and appreciation for others' successes. This mindset shift can help mitigate the effects of jealousy both personally and within their teams.
- **Role of Personal Security:** Developing a secure sense of self and reliance on God's approval above human praise is crucial. This spiritual grounding helps leaders withstand and respond appropriately to the jealousy and criticism that come with public life.
- **Historical and Biblical Context:** The chapter draws parallels between contemporary experiences of jealousy and those in the Bible, such as Joseph and Jesus, to illustrate that dealing with envy is an age-old challenge that can be navigated successfully with the right perspective and actions.

Conclusion

Jealousy is a complex issue that can severely impact individuals with influence, but with the right approach, it can be managed and overcome. By embracing strategies such as celebrating others' successes and understanding the root causes of jealousy, leaders can protect their ministries and personal lives from the corrosive effects of envy. This chapter encourages leaders to maintain their integrity and focus on their divine calling, using trials of jealousy as opportunities for growth and affirmation of their faithfulness to God's calling.

CHAPTER 6

THE WAR BETWEEN SAUL AND DAVID

Bible Verse

"The Lord has sought out a man after his own heart." - 1 Samuel 13:14 NASB

Introduction

This chapter examines the stark contrasts between King Saul and David, particularly focusing on their attitudes towards power and leadership, which significantly influenced their legacies.

Word of Wisdom

"God is looking for leaders with influence who wait for His leading and are obedient to His instructions at all costs."
Jeremiah Johnson

Main Theme

The theme centers on the dichotomy of Saul's destructive leadership and David's humble approach, serving as a spiritual and practical guide for modern leaders.

Key Points

• Saul competed with David instead of commissioning him.

• Saul prioritized his position over the presence of God.

• Saul's leadership was marred by jealousy.

• Leaders should foster growth and release rather than control.

• True leadership involves rejoicing in the success of successors.

• Jealousy in leadership leads to destruction, contrasting with leadership that builds and blesses.

Key Themes

- **Competitive vs. Commissioning Leadership:** Saul's desire to compete with David highlights a toxic leadership trait of viewing emerging leaders as threats rather than as opportunities for legacy and growth. True spiritual leaders nurture and prepare the next generation for leadership.
- **Position vs. Presence:** Saul cared more about maintaining his kingship than fostering God's presence, which

underscored his failure as a leader. Successful leaders prioritize their service to God and their community over their personal status.

- **Jealousy vs. Joyful Succession:** Saul's inability to rejoice in David's anointing illustrates the danger of jealousy in leadership. In contrast, effective leaders celebrate and support the rise of those they mentor, recognizing that true success is found in the advancement of others.
- **Destructive Outcomes of Leadership Jealousy:** Saul's jealousy led to attempts to kill David and his eventual self-destruction, showing that jealousy can be catastrophic not just for the individual but also for their entire sphere of influence.
- **Legacy of Leadership Styles:** The chapter contrasts Saul's negative legacy with David's positive impact, emphasizing that the approach to leadership directly affects one's legacy. Leaders are encouraged to adopt humility and a servant-leader model to positively influence and lead others.

Conclusion

The narrative of Saul and David offers profound lessons on leadership, particularly on the impacts of humility versus pride. By choosing to serve rather than to be served, leaders can avoid the pitfalls of jealousy and competition, fostering a healthier, more God-centered leadership style that empowers and uplifts others.

CHAPTER 7

THE DECEITFULNESS OF SIN

Bible Verse

"But your iniquities have separated you from your God..." - Isaiah 59:2 NIV

Introduction

This chapter explores the pervasive and destructive nature of sin, emphasizing its deceitfulness and the profound consequences it brings, not only to individuals but across generations.

Word of Wisdom

"Sin will take us further than we want to go, make us pay a price we do not want to pay, and keep us longer than we want to stay." Jeremiah Johnson

Main Theme

The deceitfulness of sin and its dire repercussions are examined through biblical narratives, providing a warning and wisdom on how to navigate its snares.

Key Points

• Sin's deceitfulness was first evidenced in the Garden of Eden with dire consequences for humanity.

• Sin introduces fear, shame, and contempt into human experience, alienating them from God.

• The responsibility for sin is often shifted onto others, exacerbating its effects.

• Jesus Christ's sacrifice provides a pathway out of sin's bondage.

• Awareness and recognition of sin's traps can empower individuals to live in truth and light.

• Sin's allure is contrasted with the power of the blood of Jesus to overcome its bonds.

Key Themes

- **Deceptive Allure of Sin:** Sin often appears attractive, promising pleasure and fulfillment but inevitably leads to destruction and separation from God. Understanding its deceptive nature is crucial for resisting its temptations.

- **Consequences and Awareness:** The story of Adam and Eve illustrates that sin not only brings personal shame and fear but also affects relational dynamics, highlighting the need for transparency and accountability in one's spiritual walk.
- **Role of Personal Responsibility:** The tendency to blame others for personal failings is a direct outcome of sin. Acknowledging personal responsibility is foundational for genuine repentance and spiritual growth.
- **Redemptive Power of Christ:** Christ's crucifixion and resurrection are central to overcoming sin's curse, offering believers freedom from sin's grip and enabling a life of righteousness.
- **Practical Steps to Combat Sin:** Recognizing sin's subtleties and its impact on personal and communal levels can guide individuals to seek refuge in spiritual disciplines and community accountability.

Conclusion

Sin's deceitfulness can ensnare even the most faithful, but through awareness, personal responsibility, and the redemptive work of Christ, believers can navigate its dangers and live a life aligned with God's will. This chapter calls for vigilance and fidelity to God's commands as the means to truly enjoy the freedom and life He offers.

CHAPTER 8
UPROOTING THE SPIRIT OF REJECTION

Bible Verse

"He was despised and rejected—a man of sorrows, acquainted with deepest grief. We turned our backs on him and looked the other way." - Isaiah 53:3 NLT

Introduction

This chapter delves into the universal experience of rejection, especially pronounced among those in positions of influence, and how to distinguish and overcome the debilitating spirit of rejection through biblical insights and personal reflection.

Word of Wisdom

"To be right with God has often meant to be in trouble with men." - Leonard Ravenhill

Main Theme

The spirit of rejection, often encountered by influential figures, can be devastating but is conquerable through spiritual resilience and a profound understanding of God's unconditional acceptance.

Key Points

• Rejection is a common experience for those walking in God's destiny, illustrated vividly by Daniel's trials.

• The Bible is replete with examples of godly men and women facing rejection.

• Rejection must be expected and accepted when walking in faith and executing God's will.

• The spirit of rejection manifests in various personal insecurities and defensive behaviors.

• Jesus Christ exemplified the perfect response to rejection, focusing on His relationship with God rather than human approval.

Key Themes

- **Normalization of Rejection in Destiny Fulfillment:** While rejection is typical for those in leadership or under God's favor, it should not deter one from their divine path, as demonstrated by biblical figures like Moses and David, who faced immense opposition yet persisted in their missions.

- **Symptoms of the Spirit of Rejection:** Individuals suffering from the spirit of rejection often exhibit signs like hypersensitivity to criticism, anger over benign inquiries, and an overemphasis on personal expertise, all of which stem from past hurts and a defensive stance against further emotional pain.
- **Cultural and Historical Precedence:** Throughout history, from biblical times to modern days, those who have pursued righteousness and divine purpose have often been rejected by their peers and society, a testament to the challenge of living a faith-driven life in a flawed world.
- **Strategies for Overcoming Rejection:** To effectively combat the spirit of rejection, one must engage in honest self-assessment, recognize the origin of feelings of rejection, and actively choose forgiveness and openness instead of bitterness and closure.
- **Role of Divine Acceptance in Healing:** The ultimate remedy to the spirit of rejection lies in understanding and internalizing the acceptance found in God through Jesus Christ, who, despite being the most rejected, never harbored the spirit of rejection.

Conclusion

Rejection, a common yet painful experience, holds the potential to derail one's destiny if not properly managed. By following the example set by Jesus and embracing our inherent acceptance by God, we can liberate ourselves from the spirit of rejection and fulfill our God-given purposes with integrity and joy.

CHAPTER 9

NAVIGATING SPIRITUAL WARFARE

Bible Verse

"For our struggle is not against flesh and blood, but against the rulers, against the authorities, against the powers of this dark world and against the spiritual forces of evil in the heavenly realms." - Ephesians 6:12 NIV

Introduction

This chapter explores the pervasive and intense spiritual warfare encountered by those with significant influence, highlighting that such battles are not merely human conflicts but are profoundly spiritual in nature.

Word of Wisdom

"Satan is always looking to attack and strike in strategic seasons of our

lives, especially when we are vulnerable."
Jeremiah Johnson

Main Theme

Spiritual warfare is a stark reality for individuals in influential positions, manifesting most acutely during times of birthing new ventures and transitional periods in life.

Key Points

• Significant influence invariably attracts serious spiritual warfare.

• Key life moments like the birth of Christ and Moses' infancy were marked by intense spiritual opposition.

• Spiritual warfare tends to intensify during periods of birthing and transition.

• Demonic attacks often manifest through other people or challenging circumstances.

• Specific demonic attacks target the different five-fold ministries as outlined in Ephesians 4:11-16.

Key Themes

- **Birthing and Transition as Trigger Points:** Spiritual battles often coincide with the initiation of significant new endeavors or changes in life's direction, requiring heightened spiritual vigilance and prayer during these vulnerable times.

- **Historical and Biblical Precedence:** Scriptural narratives, from Moses to Jesus, underscore that pivotal acts of God often provoke fierce opposition from spiritual adversaries, illustrating a pattern that believers might encounter today.
- **Diverse Forms of Spiritual Attacks:** Spiritual warfare can vary in form, targeting different aspects of ministry and personal life, from planting churches to transitioning into new spiritual roles, each attracting specific demonic resistances.
- **Understanding and Identifying Attacks:** Recognizing the nature of spiritual attacks, whether through a spirit of Leviathan, Jezebel, or others, is crucial for effectively countering these challenges in ministry and personal growth.
- **Practical Strategies for Overcoming Attacks:** The chapter provides practical advice for overcoming specific demonic influences, emphasizing the importance of humility, integrity, and the power of prayer in achieving victory.

Conclusion

Navigating spiritual warfare requires a deep understanding of the spiritual realm, recognizing the signs of demonic activity, and applying biblical principles and personal wisdom to stand firm against these attacks. The journey through spiritual warfare is arduous but with divine guidance and a firm resolve, one can emerge victorious, preserving the integrity of one's ministry and personal life.

CHAPTER 10

WALKING IN THE FEAR OF THE LORD

Bible Verse

"The secret of the Lord is for those who fear Him, and He will make them know His covenant." - Psalm 25:14 NASB

Introduction

This chapter underscores the profound importance of walking in the fear of the Lord, illustrating it as the key to truly understanding and harnessing the power of influence in alignment with divine approval.

Word of Wisdom

"The fear of the Lord is beauty that makes you tremble." Jeremiah Johnson

Main Theme

The fear of the Lord is presented as a transformative force that empowers individuals to align their definition of success with God's appraisal rather than human validation.

Key Points

• The fear of the Lord is essential for true spiritual confidence and peace.

• It leads to a life of security and divine protection.

• This profound reverence is linked to joy and satisfaction in God's presence.

• The early Church's growth was significantly fueled by their collective fear of the Lord.

• Personal encounters with the divine can deeply reinforce the fear of the Lord.

Key Themes

- **Definition and Effects of Fear:** The fear of the Lord involves a reverential awe and respect for God's power and majesty, which fundamentally shifts how one perceives and reacts to God's will and commands. This fear is not about terror but about recognizing God's overwhelming holiness and justice.
- **Spiritual Confidence and Joy:** Those who fear the Lord gain not only spiritual stability and confidence but also an unusual

joy in divine fellowship. This fear does not paralyze; instead, it liberates and fills the believer with a peace that transcends earthly fears.

- **Protection and Wisdom:** Living in the fear of the Lord offers a layer of protection against evil and spiritual deception. It is a guiding principle that leads to wise decisions and actions, safeguarding one's spiritual journey.
- **Influence and Multiplication:** The fear of the Lord was central to the early Church's exponential growth, suggesting that a community rooted in this fear is marked by peace and spiritual edification, leading to natural and supernatural increase.
- **Personal Transformation Through Divine Encounters:** The author's personal encounter with Jesus Christ vividly illustrates how direct experiences of God's presence can profoundly deepen the fear of the Lord, permanently transforming one's spiritual outlook and priorities.

Conclusion

Walking in the fear of the Lord is not about shrinking back in terror but stepping forward in a faith that is deeply aware of God's omnipotence and righteousness. It shapes not only personal spirituality but also how one wields influence and interacts with the world, offering a foundation of divine truth and wisdom that guides every action and decision.

DESTINY IMAGE

Destiny Image is a prophetic Christian publisher dedicated to empowering believers through Spirit-led messages. Our mission is to equip and inspire individuals to fulfill their God-given destinies by providing transformative resources that resonate with the Charismatic and Pentecostal faith.

We specialize in books, blogs, and back cover copies that reflect prophetic insights, dynamic teachings, and testimonies of faith. Our commitment to fostering spiritual growth and kingdom impact makes Destiny Image a beacon for those seeking to deepen their relationship with God and embrace their calling in the power of the Holy Spirit.

www.ingramcontent.com/pod-product-compliance
Lightning Source LLC
Chambersburg PA
CBHW052132150726
48002CB00006B/2583

9798881500757